Mia Öhrn

MACARONS, CUPCAKES & CAKE POPS

STERLING
New York

STERLING
New York

An Imprint of Sterling Publishing
387 Park Avenue South
New York, NY 10016

First Sterling edition published in 2013

Originally published in Sweden in 2011 by Natur & Kultur

Text © 2011 by Mia Öhrn
English translation © 2013 by Sterling Publishing

Graphic design and illustration by Katy Kimbell
Photography by Ulrika Pousette
Edited by Eva Kruk
English translation by Christian Gullette
Recipe consultant Wesley Martin

ISBN 978-1-4549-0576-9

Distributed in Canada by Sterling Publishing
c/o Canadian Manda Group, 165 Dufferin Street
Toronto, Ontario, Canada M6K 3H6
Distributed in the United Kingdom by GMC Distribution Services
Castle Place, 166 High Street, Lewes, East Sussex, England BN7 1XU
Distributed in Australia by Capricorn Link (Australia) Pty. Ltd.
P.O. Box 704, Windsor, NSW 2756, Australia

For information about custom editions, special sales, and premium and corporate purchases,
please contact Sterling Special Sales at 800-805-5489 or specialsales@sterlingpublishing.com.

Manufactured in China

2 4 6 8 10 9 7 5 3 1

www.sterlingpublishing.com

CONTENTS

A Sugary Sweet Silver Lining, To Life

❦ ᳁ ❦ ᳁ ❦ ᳁ ❦ ᳁ ❦

The work week takes up a large part of life. Weekdays can be dull, dreary, and full of stress, bills, and missed buses. It's something I've resigned myself to, because you can't jet-set, party, and drink champagne all day long, but there are still those little tricks that you can use to make life more fun. Drinking tap water in a wine glass, for example. Taking a bath every morning instead of a shower. And cookies, of course! They are one of those affordable luxuries that won't ruin you, but still put a silver lining in everyday life. That's what I want to accomplish with this book—to make you happier just by browsing through it, and to make your life a little more fun and glamorous both baking and eating the sweets, even if it's a dark, slushy Monday in January. So revel away in my sweetest, most luxurious, most delicious and colorful favorite desserts!

MACARON SCHOOL

Baking macarons is not especially difficult, but it is also fairly easy for things to go wrong. What characterizes a macaron is the "collar" that forms when the cookie rises from the baking sheet, making a nice and smooth top, and it is at this moment that things can go awry. Either the cookie's top cracks or it doesn't rise from the sheet and therefore never forms a collar. If you read through these tips carefully, and follow the recipe to the letter, it will go like clockwork. Use a digital scale when making macarons to ensure accurate measurements.

Meringue

There are two variations of macaron recipes: One in which a hot sugar syrup is whisked into egg whites, making a so-called "Italian meringue," and one that uses regular meringue. I think both versions work fine, but I usually make macarons using the regular meringue.

Almond

Making macarons requires almond flour, which is the same thing as ground almonds.

To make your own almond flour, blanch and peel the almonds, let them dry slightly, then grind them finely in an almond mill (I've included instructions below). Some people prefer to use a food processor, but whenever I've tried it, I get crumbly, not-quite-round macarons. I usually buy ready-made almond flour because it can be a little time-consuming to blanch, peel, and grind the almonds. You can find it at any good grocery or health food store, or online.

To get smooth and delicate macarons, it is important that you sift the flour thoroughly in a fine sieve. Weigh it carefully on a digital scale to ensure that you have the specified amount of sifted almond flour.

How to make your own almond flour for macarons

1. Weigh the almonds so that there's 2–3 ounces more than what the recipe calls for, since there will be some reduction in volume. Blanch the almonds by pouring boiling water over the almonds and let them stand for a few minutes. Drain the water and then peel the almonds by squeezing them until the skin loosens. Lay the almonds on paper towels and let them dry for at least 2 hours.

2. Grind the almonds in an almond mill, then let the powder dry some more.

3. Sift the almond flour through a fine sieve. (Do this even if using ready-made almond flour.) Weigh and verify that you have the amount of flour required for the recipe.

Egg Whites

Some recipes recommend separating the egg whites from the yolks the day before baking macarons and keeping them in the fridge overnight. This seems unnecessary to me—I always use egg whites straight from the shell, and it works well.

When whisking egg whites, it's important to use a clean, dry bowl. Stainless steel works best because it's easier to get completely clean than a plastic bowl.

Whisk the meringue using an electric mixer until it's fluffy and stiff. When making a recipe with regular meringue, you don't have to be too careful when folding the almond flour into the meringue.

Sugar

Macarons contain a little more sugar than you may like, but reducing the amount of sugar usually results in unattractive, cracked cookies. Instead, try balancing the sweetness with a slightly tart filling.

Coloring

For macarons I typically use plain liquid food coloring from the grocery store. It generally works well, but if you want a stronger color, you may end up using a little too much liquid, which can keep the cookies from rising from the baking sheet as desired. In these cases I recommend powdered food coloring.

Whatever type of coloring you use, it's important that it is designed for baking. Certain food coloring is only for marzipan and sugar paste and may lose its vibrancy in the oven, which results in pale, unappealing macarons.

Piping

Cut a sheet of baking parchment paper so that it fits the baking sheet perfectly. If the paper bends at the edges, the cookies closest to the edge will be misshapen.

Pour the macaron batter in a piping bag. I use disposable piping bags that can be found in most grocery stores, and I don't normally use a special tip, but just cut an opening that's about ⅓ inch wide. Pipe ⅛-inch-thick macarons that are about the size of a silver dollar and as round as possible.

Baking

It is important to let the unbaked cookies rest on a baking sheet for at least 45 minutes before you put them in the oven, otherwise they'll crack. You can rest them for up to two hours, but if they stand longer than that, they won't lift properly from the paper.

I usually bake macarons on the bottom rack of the oven at 275° F to make sure they are fully baked underneath but with as little brown as possible on top. In my oven this takes approximately 20 minutes, but the time varies from oven to oven. Test to see if they're done by lifting a cookie from the sheet. If it doesn't come loose from the paper, then you need to bake them a little longer. To speed things up, use a convection oven. To be on the safe side, I only bake one sheet of cookies at a time.

Let the cookies cool completely after removing them from the oven, then loosen them from the paper. If they're difficult to remove, you can put the entire paper in the freezer for a while.

Filling

I think macarons are best with lots of visible filling, but to achieve this requires a thick and creamy mixture, like buttercream frosting. I'm not too fond of buttercream, so I usually make a ganache instead. I'll make either a white chocolate ganache flavored with something tart, such as raspberry, passion fruit, or lime, or a chocolate ganache made with dark chocolate or milk chocolate. You can use a slightly less rigid filling, of course, but it might be absorbed by the cookie and not be visible.

Storage

In order to keep your macarons soft and luscious, store them in the fridge. Some people even think they taste best a day after baking. You can keep them at room temperature for several days, but they often become too brittle and crumbly.

Macarons Step-by-Step

1. Prepare the almond flour as directed on page ix.

2. Weigh the confectioner's sugar and blend with the almond flour. Sift again.

3. In a clean and dry bowl (preferably stainless steel), beat the egg whites until fluffy. Add the granulated sugar and continue beating until the egg whites form stiff peaks.

4. Fold the confectioner's sugar–almond flour mixture into the egg whites, along with the food coloring (if using).

5. Blend until you have a smooth batter. If it feels really thick and fluffy, mix it a little more, but it shouldn't be too runny either.

6. Pipe out rounds about the size of a silver dollar on two lined baking sheets. Pipe ⅛-inch-thick cookies as round and smooth as you can, then let them rest on the sheets for at least 45 minutes.

7. Preheat the oven to 275° F. Bake the cookies in batches on the oven's lowest rack for 20–25 minutes. The tops of the cookies will still be rather pale. The bottoms should come loose from the parchment paper if you try lifting them. Let the cookies cool.

8. In a small saucepan, gently heat all the filling ingredients except the food coloring (if using), stirring occasionally. Remove the pan from the heat once the filling is smooth.

9. Allow the mixture to harden in the fridge for an hour, until the cream is thick enough to pipe.

10. Pipe the filling on the flat side of half of the cookies, then assemble the macarons. They can be stored in the fridge for up to a week.

PASSION FRUIT MACARONS

Makes about 25 macarons

Passion fruit is a fantastic flavor in cookies and desserts—sweet, sour, and tasty all at once.
The pulp of the fruit makes a smooth purée, but the seeds add plenty of crispness.

Cookies

6 oz. (about 1½ cups) confectioner's sugar

4 oz. (about 1 cup plus 2 tablespoons) sifted almond flour

3 oz. egg whites (from 2–3 eggs, depending on size,
  about ⅓ cup)

2 tablespoons granulated sugar

A few drops (6 to 8) yellow food coloring

Passion Fruit Ganache

5 oz. white chocolate

2 oz. passion fruit pulp (from 2–3 fruits)

2 teaspoons honey

2 tablespoons heavy cream

A few drops of yellow food coloring (optional)

Cookies

1. Sift the weighed confectioner's sugar and almond flour together into a bowl.

2. In a clean, dry bowl (preferably stainless steel), beat the egg whites until fluffy. While beating, gradually add the granulated sugar and continue beating until the whites form stiff peaks.

3. Fold the almond flour mixture into the whites, along with the food coloring. Fold until the batter is smooth; if it is very thick and fluffy, continue folding until it loosens, but it shouldn't be too runny either.

4. Pipe rounds about the size of a silver dollar, about ⅛ inch thick and as round and smooth as you can, onto two parchment-lined baking sheets. Let the batter rest for at least 45 minutes.

5. Preheat the oven to 275°F. Bake the cookies in batches on the oven's lowest rack until the bottoms come loose from the parchment when you try lifting them, 20–25 minutes. The tops of the cookies will still be rather pale. Let the cookies cool completely on the pan.

Passion Fruit Ganache

1. Break the chocolate into small pieces.

2. Scoop the passion fruit pulp from the rind and weigh out the correct measurement.

3. In a small saucepan, gently heat all the ingredients except the food coloring, stirring occasionally. Remove the pan from the heat once the chocolate has melted and the cream appears smooth. Add a few drops yellow food coloring if you want the filling to be more colorful.

4. Allow the mixture to harden in the fridge for an hour, until the cream is thick enough to pipe.

Assembly

1. Pipe the passion fruit cream onto half the cookies to create the bottom layers.

2. Place the bottoms together with the remaining cookies to assemble the macarons. Store in the fridge for 4–5 days.

LIME AND MINT MACARONS

Makes about 25 macarons

A festive little Caipirinha in macaron form! Fresh, chic, tart, and sweet.

Cookies

6 oz. (about 1½ cups) confectioner's sugar

4 oz. (about 1 cup plus 2 tablespoons) sifted almond flour

3 oz. egg whites (from 2–3 eggs, depending on size, about ⅓ cup)

2 tablespoons granulated sugar

A few drops (6 to 8) green food coloring

Lime and Mint Cream

4 oz. white chocolate

Finely grated zest of 1 lime

1 tablespoon freshly squeezed lime juice

2 teaspoons honey

2 tablespoons heavy cream

About 10 leaves of fresh mint

Cookies

1. Sift the weighed confectioner's sugar and almond flour together into a bowl.

2. In a clean, dry bowl (preferably stainless steel), beat the egg whites until fluffy. While beating, gradually add the granulated sugar and continue beating until the whites form stiff peaks.

3. Fold the almond flour mixture into the whites, along with the food coloring. Fold until the batter is smooth; if it is very thick and fluffy, continue folding until it loosens, but it shouldn't be too runny either.

4. Pipe rounds about the size of a silver dollar, about ⅛ inch thick and as round and smooth as you can, onto two parchment-lined baking sheets. Let the batter rest for at least 45 minutes.

5. Preheat the oven to 275°F. Bake the cookies in batches on the oven's lowest rack until the bottoms come loose from the parchment when you try lifting them, 20–25 minutes. The tops of the cookies will still be rather pale. Let the cookies cool completely on the pan.

Lime and Mint Cream

1. Break the chocolate into small pieces.

2. In a small saucepan, gently heat all the chocolate, lime zest and juice, honey, and cream, stirring occasionally. Remove the pan from the heat once the chocolate has melted and the cream appears smooth. When cool, finely chop the mint and stir it into the cream.

3. Allow the mixture to harden in the fridge for an hour, until the cream is thick enough to pipe.

Assembly

1. Pipe lime and mint cream onto half the cookies to create the bottom layers.

2. Place the bottoms together with the remaining cookies to assemble the macarons. They can be stored in the fridge for up to a week.

TIP

How to Test the Jam
When you think the jam is almost ready, drop a little of it on a plate you have pre-chilled in the freezer. This will simulate the jam's consistency when it solidifies. Wait a minute and see if the drop has become solid. If it's still a little runny, cook the jam a bit longer and test again.

Raspberry Macarons

Makes about 25 macarons

I most often fill my macarons with ganache, but a thick jam also works well.
Eat the cookies with a cup of black coffee to balance the intense sweetness.

Cookies

6 oz. (about 1½ cups) confectioner's sugar

4 oz. (about 1 cup plus 2 tablespoons) sifted almond flour

3 oz. egg whites (from 2–3 eggs, depending on size,
   about ⅓ cup)

2 tablespoons granulated sugar

A few drops (6 to 8) red food coloring

Raspberry Jam

7 oz. (about 1¾ cups) raspberries, fresh or frozen and
   thawed

1.75 oz. packet powdered pectin

2 tablespoons light corn syrup

2 tablespoons freshly squeezed lemon juice

Cookies

1. Sift the weighed confectioner's sugar and almond flour together into a bowl.

2. In a clean, dry bowl (preferably stainless steel), beat the egg whites until fluffy. While beating, gradually add the granulated sugar and continue beating until the whites form stiff peaks.

3. Fold the almond flour mixture into the whites, along with the food coloring. Fold until the batter is smooth; if it is very thick and fluffy, continue folding until it loosens, but it shouldn't be too runny either.

4. Pipe rounds about the size of a silver dollar, about ⅛ inch thick and as round and smooth as you can, onto two parchment-lined baking sheets. Let the batter rest for at least 45 minutes.

5. Preheat the oven to 275°F. Bake the cookies in batches on the oven's lowest rack until the bottoms come loose from the parchment when you try lifting them, 20–25 minutes. The tops of the cookies will still be rather pale. Let the cookies cool completely on the pan.

Raspberry Jam

1. Mix the raspberries using a hand-held blender and combine with the pectin, corn syrup, and lemon juice in a wide, thick-bottomed saucepan. Bring to a boil and then simmer on medium temperature until the jam thickens. Stir occasionally and check the consistency by sampling the jam with a clean spoon.

2. Remove the pan from the heat and let the mixture cool for a while. Pour into a piping bag and place in the fridge until it has thickened and cooled.

Assembly

1. Pipe the raspberry jam onto half the cookies to create the bottom layers.

2. Place the bottoms together with the remaining cookies to assemble the macarons. They can be kept in the fridge for up to a week.

BLACK CURRANT MACARONS

Makes about 25 macarons

Black currants give a fantastic color and much-needed tartness to the filling. A seasonal treat in the past, these days you can find frozen black currants year-round in most well-stocked grocery stores.

Cookies

6 oz. (about 1½ cups) confectioner's sugar

4 oz. (about 1 cup plus 2 tablespoons) sifted almond flour

3 oz. egg whites (from 2–3 eggs, depending on size, about ⅓ cup)

2 tablespoons granulated sugar

A few drops (6 to 8) red and blue food coloring

Black Currant Cream

4 oz. black currants, fresh or frozen and thawed

5 oz. white chocolate

2 teaspoons honey

2 tablespoons heavy cream

Cookies

1. Sift the weighed confectioner's sugar and almond flour together into a bowl.
2. In a clean, dry bowl (preferably stainless steel), beat the egg whites until fluffy. While beating, gradually add the granulated sugar and continue beating until the whites form stiff peaks.
3. Fold the almond flour mixture into the whites, along with the food coloring. Fold until the batter is smooth; if it is very thick and fluffy, continue folding until it loosens, but it shouldn't be too runny either.
4. Pipe rounds about the size of a silver dollar, about ⅛ inch thick and as round and smooth as you can, onto two parchment-lined baking sheets. Let the batter rest for at least 45 minutes.

5. Preheat the oven to 275°F. Bake the cookies in batches on the oven's lowest rack until the bottoms come loose from the parchment when you try lifting them, 20–25 minutes. The tops of the cookies will still be rather pale. Let the cookies cool completely on the pan.

Black Currant Cream

1. Mash the currants well and pass them through a sieve in order to separate and remove the skin and seeds from the flesh. Weigh out 2 ounces.
2. Break the chocolate into small pieces.
3. In a small saucepan, gently heat all the ingredients, stirring occasionally. Remove the pan from the heat once the chocolate has melted and the cream appears smooth.
4. Allow the mixture to harden in the fridge for an hour, until the cream is thick enough to pipe.

Assembly

1. Pipe the black currant cream onto half the cookies to create the bottom layers.
2. Place the bottoms together with the remaining cookies to assemble the macarons. They can be kept in the fridge for up to a week.

HAZELNUT MACARONS WITH PEAR COGNAC GANACHE

Makes about 25 macarons

A dark chocolate filling makes these cookies especially delicious and a little less sweet than the typical macaron. Instead of pear cognac, you can flavor the filling with rum, whiskey, Baileys Irish Cream, or any liqueur you happen to have on hand.

Cookies

1 cup shelled, peeled hazelnuts, toasted

6 oz. (about 1 1/2 cups) confectioner's sugar

3 oz. egg whites (from 2–3 eggs, depending on size, about 1/3 cup)

2 tablespoons granulated sugar

Pear Cognac Ganache

4 oz. dark chocolate

1/2 cup heavy cream

1 teaspoon honey

2 teaspoons butter, room temperature

1 1/2 tablespoons pear cognac, or similar cognac or liqueur

Cookies

1. Grind the hazelnuts in an almond mill. Sift the flour and measure 4 ounces hazelnut flour; reserve remaining for another use. Sift the weighed confectioner's sugar and hazelnut flour together into a bowl.
2. In a clean, dry bowl (preferably stainless steel), beat the egg whites until fluffy. While beating, gradually add the granulated sugar and continue beating until the whites form stiff peaks.
3. Fold the hazelnut flour mixture into the whites, until the batter is smooth; if it is very thick and fluffy, continue folding until it loosens, but it shouldn't be too runny either.

4. Pipe rounds about the size of a silver dollar, about 1/8 inch thick and as round and smooth as you can, onto two parchment-lined baking sheets. Let the batter rest for at least 45 minutes.
5. Preheat the oven to 275°F. Bake the cookies in batches on the oven's lowest rack until the bottoms come loose from the parchment when you try lifting them, 20–25 minutes. The tops of the cookies will still be rather pale. Let the cookies cool completely on the pan.

Pear Cognac Ganache

1. Finely chop the chocolate.
2. In a small saucepan, mix together the cream and honey and bring to a boil. Remove from heat and quickly add the chocolate. Stir until the chocolate is melted, then add the butter. Mix until smooth and shiny, then add the liqueur.
3. Allow the ganache to cool, preferably 2–3 hours at room temperature, but if you're in a hurry, you can put it in the fridge for about 15 minutes.

Assembly

1. Pipe the ganache onto half the cookies to create the bottom layers.
2. Place the bottoms together with the remaining cookies to assemble the macarons. They can be kept in the fridge for up to a week.

TIP

Peeled, lightly toasted hazelnuts are available in many supermarkets, but if you can't find them, don't hesitate to use ordinary hazelnuts and roast and shell them yourself.

CHOCOLATE MACARONS WITH COFFEE GANACHE

Makes about 25 macarons

After you've mastered the art of making macarons, it's time to make them even more stylish with sprinkles and chocolate decorations.

Cookies

6 oz. (about 1½ cups) confectioner's sugar

3 oz. (about 1 cup) sifted almond flour

2 tablespoons cocoa powder

3 oz. egg whites (from 2–3 eggs, depending on size, about ⅓ cup)

2 tablespoons granulated sugar

Coffee Ganache

5 oz. dark chocolate

⅔ cup heavy cream

1 teaspoon honey

2 tablespoons instant coffee granules

2 tablespoons butter, room temperature

Decorations

3 oz. white chocolate

Sprinkles and chocolate-covered coffee beans

Cookies

1. Sift the weighed confectioner's sugar, almond flour, and cocoa together into a bowl.
2. In a clean, dry bowl (preferably stainless steel), beat the egg whites until fluffy. While beating, gradually add the granulated sugar and continue beating until the whites form stiff peaks.
3. Fold the almond flour mixture into the whites. Fold until the batter is smooth; if it is very thick and fluffy, continue folding until it loosens, but it shouldn't be too runny either.
4. Pipe rounds about the size of a silver dollar, about ⅛ inch thick and as round and smooth as you can, onto two parchment-lined baking sheets. Let the batter rest for at least 45 minutes.
5. Preheat the oven to 275°F. Bake the cookies in batches on the oven's lowest rack until the bottoms come loose from the parchment when you try lifting them, 20–25 minutes. The tops of the cookies will still be rather pale. Let the cookies cool completely on the pan.

Coffee Ganache

1. Finely chop the chocolate.
2. In a small saucepan, stir together the cream and honey and bring to a boil. Remove from the heat and quickly whisk in the instant coffee followed by the chocolate. Mix until smooth and glossy, then add the butter.
3. Allow the mixture to cool and thicken at room temperature for 2–3 hours. If you are in a hurry, you can set the ganache in the fridge for about 15 minutes.

Assembly

1. Pipe coffee ganache onto half the cookies to create the bottom layers.
2. Place the bottoms together with the remaining cookies to assemble the macarons.
3. Carefully melt the white chocolate, stirring often.
4. Decorate the cookies with chocolate, sprinkles, and chocolate-covered coffee beans. Place on a tray lined with waxed paper and let them harden in the fridge. They can be kept in the fridge for up to a week.

TIP

Performing a ball test

A ball test simulates the consistency of the caramel when it has cooled. To perform one, drop a bit of the mixture in a glass filled with ice-cold water. Wait a few seconds and then see if you can form the mixture into a soft ball. If the caramel is still too runny, simply cook it a little longer.

CHOCOLATE MACARONS WITH SALTED CARAMEL

Makes about 25 macarons

*A little salt in sweet cookies is often the secret ingredient that makes them so heavenly good.
Prepare the caramel a day before baking the cookies.*

Cookies

6 oz. (about 1½ cups) confectioner's sugar

3 oz. (about 1 cup) sifted almond flour

2 tablespoons cocoa powder

3 oz. egg whites (from 2–3 eggs, depending on size,
 about ⅓ cup)

2 tablespoons granulated sugar

Salted Caramel

⅓ cup granulated sugar

¼ cup light corn syrup

¼ cup water

⅓ cup heavy cream

5 tablespoons butter, room temperature

About 1 teaspoon flaked salt

Cookies

1. Sift the weighed confectioner's sugar, almond flour, and cocoa together into a bowl.

2. In a clean, dry bowl (preferably stainless steel), beat the egg whites until fluffy. While beating, gradually add the granulated sugar and continue beating until the whites form stiff peaks.

3. Fold the almond flour mixture into the whites. Fold until the batter is smooth; if it is very thick and fluffy, continue folding until it loosens, but it shouldn't be too runny either.

4. Pipe rounds about the size of a silver dollar, about ⅛ inch thick and as round and smooth as you can, onto two parchment-lined baking sheets. Let the batter rest for at least 45 minutes.

5. Preheat the oven to 275°F. Bake the cookies in batches on the oven's lowest rack until the bottoms come loose from the parchment when you try lifting them, 20–25 minutes. The tops of the cookies will still be rather pale. Let the cookies cool completely on the pan.

Salted Caramel

1. Blend the sugar, syrup, and water in a fairly wide and thick-bottomed saucepan. Bring to a boil and then simmer until the sugar syrup becomes golden brown (do not stir). Tilt the pan if necessary for even caramelization.

2. Stir in the cream (it may pop and sputter a bit, but this is normal) and then the butter. Let it cook slowly a few minutes until the caramel thickens slightly. Check the consistency of the caramel with a ball test (see instructions to the left). It should be soft, but not too runny.

3. Remove from the heat and stir in the flaked salt. Let the caramel cool completely, preferably overnight at room temperature, although if you're in a hurry you can put it in the fridge. Don't touch the caramel while it cools.

Assembly

1. Pipe the caramel on the bottom halves of the cookies. If you desire, sprinkle extra flaked salt over them before putting them together with the remaining cookies to assemble the macarons. They can be kept in the fridge for up to a week.

CARDAMOM MACARONS WITH MILK CHOCOLATE GANACHE

Makes about 25 macarons

My favorite macaron in the whole book! I can't get enough cardamom—in buns, cream puffs, coffee, and, yes, even macarons.

Cookies

- *6 oz. (about 1½ cups) confectioner's sugar*
- *4 oz. (about 1 cup plus 2 tablespoons) sifted almond flour*
- *1 teaspoon ground cardamom*
- *3 oz. egg whites (from 2–3 eggs, depending on size, about ⅓ cup)*
- *2 tablespoons granulated sugar*

Milk Chocolate Ganache

- *5 oz. milk chocolate*
- *⅓ cup heavy cream*
- *1 teaspoon honey*
- *½ teaspoon ground cinnamon*
- *1 tablespoon butter, room temperature*

Decorations

- *2 oz. dark chocolate*

Cookies

1. Sift the weighed confectioner's sugar, almond flour, and cardamom together into a bowl.
2. In a clean, dry bowl (preferably stainless steel), beat the egg whites until fluffy. While beating, gradually add the granulated sugar and continue beating until the whites form stiff peaks.
3. Fold the almond flour mixture into the whites. Fold until the batter is smooth; if it is very thick and fluffy, continue folding until it loosens, but it shouldn't be too runny either.
4. Pipe rounds about the size of a silver dollar, about ⅛ inch thick and as round and smooth as you can, onto two parchment-lined baking sheets. Let the batter rest for at least 45 minutes.
5. Preheat the oven to 275°F. Bake the cookies in batches on the oven's lowest rack until the bottoms come loose from the parchment when you try lifting them, 20–25 minutes. The tops of the cookies will still be rather pale. Let the cookies cool completely on the pan.

Milk Chocolate Ganache

1. Finely chop the milk chocolate.
2. In a small saucepan, mix the honey and cinnamon with the cream and bring to a boil. Remove from heat and quickly add the chocolate. Stir until the chocolate has melted, then add the butter and mix until fully incorporated. Let the ganache cool and thicken at room temperature for about 3 hours. If you're in a hurry, you can set it in the fridge for a while, but check often to make sure it doesn't get too hard.

Assembly

1. Pipe the milk chocolate ganache onto half the cookies to create the bottom layers.
2. Place the bottoms together with the remaining cookies to assemble the macarons.
3. Carefully melt the dark chocolate and pipe or drizzle over the cookies, allowing them to harden in the fridge. The cookies can be stored in the fridge for up to a week.

Licorice Macarons

Makes about 25 macarons

I know a lot of people who are basically addicted to licorice macarons—quite an expensive habit in the long run. For the sake of your pocketbook, it's helpful to make your own. To get a really dark color, powdered food coloring works best.

Cookies

6 oz. (about 1½ cups) confectioner's sugar

4 oz. (about 1 cup plus 2 tablespoons) sifted almond flour

About 1 teaspoon black powdered food coloring

3 oz. egg whites (from 2–3 eggs, depending on size, about ⅓ cup)

2 tablespoons granulated sugar

Licorice Ganache

5 oz. dark chocolate

⅔ cup heavy cream

1 teaspoon honey

1½ tablespoons licorice powder or 2 teaspoons licorice (anise) extract

2 tablespoons butter, room temperature

Cookies

1. Sift the weighed confectioner's sugar, almond flour, and powdered food coloring together into a bowl.
2. In a clean, dry bowl (preferably stainless steel), beat the egg whites until fluffy. While beating, gradually add the granulated sugar and continue beating until the whites form stiff peaks.
3. Fold the almond flour mixture into the whites. Fold until the batter is smooth; if it is very thick and fluffy, continue folding until it loosens, but it shouldn't be too runny either.
4. Pipe rounds about the size of a silver dollar, about ⅛ inch thick and as round and smooth as you can, onto two parchment-lined baking sheets. Let the batter rest for at least 45 minutes.

5. Preheat the oven to 275°F. Bake the cookies in batches on the oven's lowest rack until the bottoms come loose from the parchment when you try lifting them, 20–25 minutes. The tops of the cookies will still be rather pale. Let the cookies cool completely on the pan.

Licorice Ganache

1. Finely chop the chocolate.
2. In a small saucepan, mix the honey and licorice powder with the cream and bring to a boil. (If using extract, stir into the ganache after the butter.) Remove from heat and quickly add the chocolate. Stir until the chocolate has melted, then add the butter and mix until fully incorporated. Let the ganache cool and thicken at room temperature for about 3 hours. If you're in a hurry, you can set it in the fridge for a while, but check often to make sure it doesn't get too hard.

Assembly

1. Pipe the licorice ganache onto half the cookies to create the bottom layers.
2. Place the bottoms together with the remaining cookies to assemble the macarons. They can be kept in the fridge for up to a week.

MACARON LOLLIPOPS WITH STRAWBERRY GANACHE

Makes about 20 lollipops

Cookies

6 oz. (about 1½ cups) confectioner's sugar

4 oz. (about 1 cup plus 2 tablespoons) sifted almond flour

3 oz. egg whites (from 2–3 eggs, depending on size, about ⅓ cup)

2 tablespoons granulated sugar

A few drops (6 to 8) red food coloring

Strawberry Ganache

4 oz. white chocolate

4 oz. strawberries (about 6 whole), fresh or frozen and thawed

Finely grated zest of 1 lemon

2 teaspoons honey

2 tablespoons heavy cream

Decorations

1 oz. white chocolate, melted (to fasten the lollipops to the sticks)

Edible pearl luster spray (optional)

Lollipop sticks

Cookies

1. Sift the weighed confectioner's sugar and almond flour together into a bowl.
2. In a clean, dry bowl (preferably stainless steel), beat the egg whites until fluffy. While beating, gradually add the granulated sugar and continue beating until the whites form stiff peaks.
3. Fold the almond flour mixture into the whites, along with the food coloring. Fold until the batter is smooth; if it is very thick and fluffy, continue folding until it loosens, but it shouldn't be too runny either.
4. Pipe hearts about the size of a silver dollar, about ⅛ inch thick and as round and smooth as you can, onto two parchment-lined baking sheets. Let the batter rest for at least 45 minutes.
5. Preheat the oven to 275°F. Bake the cookies in batches on the oven's lowest rack until the bottoms come loose from the parchment when you try lifting them, 20–25 minutes. The tops of the cookies will still be rather pale. Let the cookies cool completely on the pan.

Strawberry Ganache

1. Mash the strawberries well, then bring them to a boil in a small saucepan. Simmer for 5–10 minutes, or until about half the liquid has evaporated. Weigh and measure 2 ounces of strawberry reduction.
2. Break the chocolate into small pieces.
3. In a small saucepan, gently heat all the ingredients, stirring occasionally. Remove the pan from the heat once the chocolate has melted and the cream appears smooth.
4. Allow the mixture to harden in the fridge for an hour, until the cream is thick enough to pipe.

Assembly

1. Pipe the strawberry cream onto half the cookies to create the bottom layers.
2. Dip one end of the lollipop stick in a little melted white chocolate. Place the sticks on top of the cookies with filling and then cover with the top layer cookies. Let it harden in the fridge.
3. Spray the lollipops with edible luster dust. Macaron pops can be kept in the fridge for up to a week.

ISPAHAN

Makes about 25 macarons

This beautiful cookie, named after a Middle-Eastern rose and the Iranian city of Isfahen, is flavored with rose water and adorned with petals. The original was created by master French pastry chef Pierre Hermé.

Cookies

6 oz. (about 1½ cups) confectioner's sugar

4 oz. (about 1 cup plus 2 tablespoons) sifted almond flour

3 oz. egg whites (from 2–3 eggs, depending on size, about ⅓ cup)

2 tablespoons granulated sugar

A few drops (6 to 8) red food coloring

Lychee and Rose Cream

6 lychees, fresh or canned

4 oz. white chocolate

2 teaspoons honey

2 tablespoons heavy cream

¼ teaspoon rose water

About 2½ cups fresh raspberries

Decoration

Rose petals

Cookies

1. Sift the weighed confectioner's sugar and almond flour together into a bowl.
2. In a clean, dry bowl (preferably stainless steel), beat the egg whites until fluffy. While beating, gradually add the granulated sugar and continue beating until the whites form stiff peaks.
3. Fold the almond flour mixture into the whites, along with the food coloring. Fold until the batter is smooth; if it is very thick and fluffy, continue folding until it loosens, but it shouldn't be too runny either.

4. Pipe rounds about the size of a silver dollar, about ⅛ inch thick and as round and smooth as you can, onto two parchment-lined baking sheets. Let the batter rest for at least 45 minutes.
5. Preheat the oven to 275°F. Bake the cookies in batches on the oven's lowest rack until the bottoms come loose from the parchment when you try lifting them, 20–25 minutes. The tops of the cookies will still be rather pale. Let the cookies cool completely on the pan.

Lychee and Rose Cream

1. Peel the lychees (if using fresh) and remove the cores. In a blender, puree the lychees until smooth. Measure 2 ounces puree for the cream. Reserve remaining lychee puree for another use.
2. Break the chocolate into small pieces.
3. Gently heat all the ingredients for the cream, except for the rose water, in a small saucepan. Stir occasionally and pull the pan from the heat once the chocolate has melted and the cream appears nice and smooth. Flavor with rose water, and add more if desired. Let it harden in the fridge for an hour. The cream should be thick enough to pipe.

Assembly

1. Pipe the lychee and rose onto half the cookies to create the bottom layers. Decorate with fresh raspberries.
2. Place the bottoms together with the remaining cookies to assemble the macarons. They will keep in the fridge for 1–2 days. Decorate with a rose petal just before serving.

CHOCOLATE GANACHE

Chocolate ganache is tasty, attractive, and useful in so many ways. In its simplest form, it is nothing more than melted chocolate mixed with heavy cream that solidifies into a smooth cream. Chocolate ganache can be flavored with spices, fruits, and berries, or liqueurs and coffee. It is used as a filling for macarons and tarts, as well as icing, topping, and decorations for cupcakes, or as a base for hot chocolate drinks.

☙ Chocolate ganache can be made from dark, white, or milk chocolate. The consistency is usually slightly runnier when made with white or milk chocolate instead of dark chocolate, but this can be fixed by adjusting the amount of heavy cream or increasing the amount of chocolate.

☙ If things don't go well, the ganache mixture can curdle, which means that the fat separates and the texture gets grainy and dull. There are many reasons why a ganache can separate. It might be because it is too rich, too light, or too cold, or that you have added ingredients that are too acidic. It's difficult to save a ganache that has separated, but you can try to mix it with a hand blender. My ganache recipes often contain a small amount of honey,

which both prevents the risk of the ganache separating and improves consistency. Keep in mind that the cream must be very hot when you mix the ganache. Try not to stir it too rapidly. Mix it with care or use a hand blender.

☙ I make ganache most often with a chocolate that contains about 55% cocoa so that the flavor comes through better. If you use a darker chocolate it could easily overwhelm the flavor, but this is a minor point. Feel free to use darker chocolate if you prefer.

☙ To get the best consistency, let the ganache stand at room temperature overnight. If you are eager to use it, you can harden it in the fridge for a few hours.

Orange Ganache Biskvier

Makes about 30 small cookies

Chocolate flavored with orange is usually a combination that one either loves or loathes, but I have trouble believing that someone could say no to one of these little heart-shaped, orange ganache biskvier.

Bottoms

1¼ cups (10 oz.) almond paste

1 egg white

Ganache

7 oz. dark chocolate

½ cup heavy cream

2 tablespoons butter

1 tablespoon freshly squeezed orange juice

Finely grated zest of 1 orange

Icing

9 oz. dark chocolate

Cookies

1. Preheat the oven to 350° F.
2. In a food processor, blend the almond paste and egg white into a smooth batter.
3. Fill a disposable piping bag with the batter. Cut a hole in the bag and pipe small, heart-shaped bottoms for the cookies, with ample room between them, on two baking sheets lined with parchment paper.
4. Bake on the middle rack for 8–10 minutes, or until the bottoms are slightly brown. Let cool.

Ganache

1. Finely chop the chocolate.
2. In a small saucepan, mix the cream, butter, orange juice, and orange zest and bring to a boil.
3. Remove from the heat, add the chopped chocolate and stir until it melts. Mix to a smooth and shiny ganache paste. Let the ganache cool and then chill in the fridge.

Assembly

1. Loosen the cookies from the sheets and place them on a tray with the flat side facing up.
2. Fill a piping bag with the ganache and pipe a heart shape on every cookie. Let the biskvier harden in the fridge for 20–30 minutes.
3. Break the dark chocolate into smaller pieces and carefully melt in a microwave or water bath.
4. Dip the tops of the biskviers in the melted chocolate. Let harden in the fridge. Biskviers will keep in the fridge 1–2 weeks; freezing them also works well.

Raspberry Ganache Bars

Makes about 35 small bars

If I was only able to use one berry in my cookies, I would choose the raspberry—sweet, tart, tasty, and wonderful! Especially with dark chocolate. Decorating with chocolate can take some time, so if you choose to skip it, the bars will turn out just fine.

Bottom

⅔ cup granulated sugar
⅔ cup flour
1 teaspoon baking powder
¼ teaspoon salt
7 tablespoons chilled butter
2 small egg yolks

Raspberry Ganache

14 oz. dark chocolate
2 cups raspberry purée (fresh or frozen and thawed raspberries that have been pureed and strained through a sieve)
1 cup heavy cream
2 tablespoons honey
5 tablespoons butter
2 tablespoons raspberry liqueur

Decoration

4 oz. dark chocolate
About 1¼ cups fresh raspberries

Crust

1. Preheat the oven to 400°F. Line a 8 x 11 inch baking dish with parchment paper.
2. Mix the dry ingredients in a food processor. Add the butter and mix together into crumbles.
3. Add the egg yolks and blend quickly into a dough.
4. Press the dough into an even layer in the pan and bake on the center rack of the oven for 10 minutes, or until golden brown. Allow to cool.

Raspberry Ganache

1. Finely chop the chocolate and place in a bowl.
2. In a small saucepan, bring the raspberry purée, cream, honey, and butter to a boil. Remove from the heat.
3. Pour the hot mixture over the chocolate and mix with a hand blender or in a food processor until smooth. Add the raspberry liqueur and pour the ganache in the pan over the bottom crust. Let harden in the fridge for at least 3–4 hours.
4. Remove from the pan and cut it into pieces. The easiest way to do this is by rinsing a knife under hot water and drying it between each cut. The bars can be stored in the refrigerator for up to a week.

Assembly

1. Cut waxed paper or acetate into 4 x 4-inch pieces.
2. Carefully melt the chocolate and drizzle or pipe it diagonally on the paper or plastic sheets. Roll up the sheets and put them in thin, tall glasses. Secure the seam with a paper clip and place in refrigerator for 20–30 minutes, then remove the chocolate from the paper.
3. Decorate the bars with a fresh raspberry and the chocolate curls.

ALMOND BRITTLE WITH RUM GANACHE

Makes about 25 pieces

Crunchy and creamy with almonds and chocolate! The brittle sets quickly, so keep up the pace as you roll and cut it. And watch your paws because it's burning hot!

Rum Ganache

5 oz. dark chocolate

½ cup heavy cream

1 teaspoon honey

2 tablespoons butter, room temperature

1½ tablespoons rum

Almond Brittle

1⅔ cups granulated sugar

1 tablespoon butter

⅓ teaspoon salt

¾ cup sliced blanched almonds

Decoration

Sugar pearls

Rum Ganache

1. Finely chop the chocolate.
2. In a small saucepan, stir together the cream and honey and bring to a boil. Remove from heat and quickly add the chocolate. Stir until the chocolate is melted, then add the butter. Mix until smooth and shiny, then add the rum.
3. Allow the ganache to cool, preferably 2–3 hours at room temperature, but if you're in a hurry, you can put it in the fridge for about 15 minutes.

Almond Brittle

1. Prepare to make the brittle by setting out a rimless cookie sheet, two sheets of parchment paper, and a rolling pin.
2. Measure the sugar into a heavy-bottomed saucepan. Let the sugar melt at a relatively high temperature on the stove. Try not to stir it, although a little poke now and then is okay. Reduce the heat when the sugar starts to brown, and continue heating until it is golden brown. Stir in the butter and salt.
3. Remove from heat and quickly add the almonds. Pour the brittle on one cookie sheet lined with paper and cover with the second piece of paper. Roll out the brittle into thin sheets. Remove the top paper and quickly cut the brittle into small, rectangles while still warm. Allow to cool.

Assembly

1. Pipe the rum ganache on half of the brittle pieces with a rippled or scalloped piping tip. Place a second piece of brittle on top and apply another layer of ganache.
2. Decorate with sugar pearls. The bars can be stored at room temperature for up to 2 days, or in an airtight jar for up to one week.

About Cupcakes

These days cupcake baking cups and liners are available in all sorts of colors and styles. Not all hold their shape and color in the oven, however, and some can become greasy or even burn. Therefore it's important to find good liners.

☞ For tall cupcakes, bake them in double-size baking cups or put paper cups in a cupcake tin. Cupcakes with a stately, piped top are gorgeous, but you may decide that less is more. If you decide to use less frosting, you can halve the amount of frosting in a recipe that calls for a hefty peak such as the Strawberry Cupcake on p. 38.

☞ Before you've frosted your cupcakes, you can keep them in a plastic bag at room temperature for 24 hours, or freeze them. After they're frosted, they'll last at room temperature for a few hours, or in the fridge for 24 hours.

ON PIPING

Piping is a technique that takes a little practice, so don't give up if it feels a little tricky in the beginning. The piping tools you'll use will depend on what you want to pipe. Take a peek at some online videos to get additional tips on piping.

When piping decorations and small details with melted chocolate or icing, I fold wax or parchment paper into a little piping bag. For icing and ganache decorations, I use a disposable piping bag with small decorative piping tips. See p. 29

for the results. I use a disposable piping bag without a tip when piping macarons. I pipe cream or topping on cupcakes through a disposable piping bag with a decorative tip, preferably star or flower-shaped.

BLUEBERRY CUPCAKES

Makes 14–18 cupcakes

Decorating cakes with fresh flowers is my best trick for making them irresistibly beautiful. Few flowers are poisonous, but always consult a guidebook about flowers and plants to be sure, and use organically grown flowers. My favorites are lilacs, roses, violets, lavender, or, as used here, chrysanthemums. Vanilla powder is made from finely ground vanilla beans, which can be purchased at gourmet grocery stores or online, but if you can't find them, use vanilla essence.

Cupcakes

1½ cups flour

2 teaspoons baking powder

½ teaspoon vanilla powder or 1 teaspoon vanilla essence

3 large eggs

¾ cup granulated sugar

⅔ cup milk

5 tablespoons butter, melted

3 oz. white chocolate, coarsely chopped

About ½ cup blueberries, fresh or frozen and thawed

Frosting

⅓ cup blueberries, fresh or frozen and thawed

⅓ cup confectioner's sugar

10 oz. cream cheese

½ cup heavy cream

Decoration

Blueberries

White chocolate chips

Fresh, edible flowers

Cupcakes

1. Preheat the oven to 350° F.
2. Mix together the flour, baking powder, and vanilla powder.
3. Using an electric mixer, beat the eggs and sugar until fluffy.
4. Sift the flour mixture into the egg batter a little at a time, alternating with adding the milk and melted butter. Beat together until it becomes a smooth batter.
5. Distribute the batter into the cupcake liners and sprinkle chocolate and blueberries over them (if using frozen berries, there's no need to thaw them first). Bake in the oven on the middle rack for approximately 25 minutes. Allow to cool.

Topping

1. Mix the blueberries with a hand blender. Pass the puree through a sieve to get it completely smooth.
2. Whisk the confectioner's sugar and blueberry puree in with the cream cheese. Add the cream, a little at a time, beating with an electric mixer until it becomes a fluffy frosting.
3. Pipe or spread the frosting on the cupcakes and decorate with blueberries, white chocolate, and fresh, edible flowers.

Rocky Road Cupcakes

Makes about 12 cupcakes

When I was little, my grandmother and grandfather treated me to rocky road ice cream—a wonderfully memorable treat. Here, the nuts, marshmallow, and chocolate are rolled into a tasty cupcake.

Cupcakes

1½ sticks butter

7 oz. dark chocolate

4 large eggs

¾ cup granulated sugar

⅔ cup flour

½ cup cocoa

1 teaspoon baking powder

¼ teaspoon salt

½ cup mini marshmallows

About ½ cup pecan halves

Topping

7 oz. dark chocolate

1 cup heavy cream

2 teaspoons honey

2 tablespoons butter, room temperature

Decoration

Mini marshmallows

Pecans

Cupcakes

1. Preheat the oven to 350° F.
2. Melt the butter in a saucepan. Break the chocolate into pieces and melt it in the pan with the butter at low temperature. Mix until smooth, then pull the pan off the heat and let cool slightly.
3. Lightly beat the eggs with the sugar, then stir in the chocolate mixture.
4. Combine the flour, cocoa, baking powder, and salt, and add to the batter. Mix until smooth.
5. Divide the batter into cupcake liners and sprinkle the pecans and marshmallows over the batter.
6. Bake on the oven's lowest rack for 15–20 minutes for a slightly underbaked, gooey middle. Allow to cool.

Topping

1. Finely chop the chocolate. Bring the cream and honey to a boil, then pull the pan from the heat and quickly mix the chopped chocolate into the hot cream. Stir until all the chocolate has melted.
2. Add the butter and mix until smooth. Let the frosting harden at room temperature, preferably until the next day. Cool it in the fridge if you're in a hurry, but watch closely so it doesn't get too hard.
3. Spread chocolate frosting on each cupcake and decorate with mini-marshmallows and pecans.

LICORICE CUPCAKES

Makes about 12 cupcakes

I love all sweets except for licorice, so this cake is an homage to all you licorice lovers out there. Licorice powder can be purchased at spice shops or online.

Cupcakes

- *½ cup flour*
- *½ cup cocoa*
- *2 tablespoons licorice powder or 2 teaspoons licorice (anise) extract*
- *1 teaspoon baking powder*
- *3 large eggs*
- *¾ cup granulated sugar*
- *½ cup milk*
- *7 tablespoons butter, melted*

Topping

- *10 oz. dark chocolate*
- *1¼ cups heavy cream*
- *1 tablespoon honey*
- *1 tablespoon licorice powder or 1½ teaspoons licorice extract*
- *2 tablespoons butter, room temperature*

Decoration

- *Striped licorice, or similar licorice candies*

Cupcakes

1. Preheat the oven to 350° F.
2. Mix together the flour, cocoa, licorice powder, and baking powder. (If using licorice extract, add it to the eggs.)
3. Using an electric mixer, beat the eggs and sugar until fluffy.
4. Sift the flour mixture into the egg batter a little at a time, alternating with adding the milk and melted butter. Beat together until it becomes a smooth batter.
5. Distribute the batter into the cupcake liners and bake in the oven on the center rack for approximately 25 minutes. Allow to cool.

Topping

1. Finely chop the chocolate.
2. Bring the cream to a boil with the honey and licorice powder, then pull the pan from the heat and quickly mix the chopped chocolate into the hot cream. Stir until all the chocolate has melted.
3. Add the butter and mix until smooth. Let the frosting harden at room temperature, preferably until the next day. Cool it in the fridge if you're in a hurry, but watch closely so it doesn't get too hard.
4. Pipe a dollop of ganache on top each cupcake and decorate with striped licoric.

STRAWBERRY CUPCAKES

Makes about 16 cupcakes

A real summer's dream cupcake, in which the fluffy mascarpone topping hides a trove of strawberries.

Cupcakes

1 ½ cups flour

2 teaspoons baking powder

½ teaspoons vanilla powder or 2 teaspoons vanilla sugar

3 large eggs

¾ cup granulated sugar

Finely grated zest of 1 lemon

⅔ cup milk

5 tablespoons butter, melted

Filling

1 cup (5 oz.) strawberries, fresh or frozen and thawed

Topping

1 ¾ cups (9 oz.) strawberries, fresh or frozen and thawed

2 tablespoons granulated sugar

18 oz. mascarpone cheese

¾ cups heavy cream

Cupcakes

1. Preheat the oven to 350° F.
2. Mix together the flour, baking powder, and vanilla powder.
3. Using an electric mixer, beat the eggs, sugar, and lemon zest until fluffy.
4. Sift the flour mixture into the egg batter a little at a time, alternating with adding the milk and melted butter. Beat together until it becomes a smooth batter.
5. Distribute the batter into the cupcake liners. Bake on the center rack of the oven for approximately 25 minutes. Allow to cool.

Filling

1. Scoop out some of the insides of each cupcake and crumble it coarsely in a bowl.
2. Mash the strawberries and mix them with the crumbs.
3. Refill each cupcake with the crumb-strawberry mixture.

Topping

1. In a saucepan, mash the strawberries with the granulated sugar. Bring to a boil, then simmer on low heat for 10–15 minutes to reduce the liquid slightly. Allow to cool completely.
2. Using an electric mixer, whip the mascarpone and cream together until fluffy.
3. To get a "rippled" effect, drizzle the strawberry puree along the inside edges of a piping bag. Pour the whipped mascarpone into the bag and pipe on top of the cupcakes.

candy cane cupcakes

Makes about 12–14 cupcakes

Perfect for the holidays, or any time of the year, peppermint and cream is a match made in heaven.

Cupcakes

10 tablespoons butter

¾ cup granulated sugar

3 oz. candy cane

1⅔ cups flour

1 teaspoon baking powder

⅔ cup heavy cream

2 large eggs

Topping

¼ cup confectioner's sugar

7 oz. cream cheese

⅓ cup heavy cream

⅓ teaspoon peppermint essence or flavoring

Decoration

Small peppermint sticks or candy canes

Cupcakes

1. Preheat the oven to 350° F.
2. Melt the butter and stir in the sugar.
3. Finely crush the candy canes and mix them with the flour and baking powder. Stir into the butter mixture, along with the cream and eggs.
4. Divide the batter into cupcake liners. Bake in the center of the oven for about 20 minutes. Allow to cool.

Topping

1. Stir the confectioner's sugar into the cream cheese. Add the cream and peppermint flavoring. Taste and adjust the amount of peppermint to your liking.
2. Using an electric mixer, whip the topping until fluffy.
3. Spread the topping on the cupcakes and decorate with small candy canes or peppermint sticks.

APPLE CUPCAKES

Makes about 10 cupcakes

Nothing is as comforting as apple cake with vanilla sauce, here in cupcake form with vanilla yogurt cream as the topping, and soft little caramels intermingled with the apples as the filling.

Cupcakes

3 large eggs

⅔ cup granulated sugar

1½ cups flour

1 teaspoon baking powder

¼ teaspoon salt

1 tablespoon vanilla sugar

⅔ cup milk

7 tablespoons butter, melted

2 medium apples

1 teaspoon ground cinnamon

6–8 soft caramels

Topping

8 oz. vanilla flavored whole milk yogurt

¾ cups heavy cream

Decoration

Sugar flowers

Cupcakes

1. Preheat the oven to 350° F.
2. Mix the eggs with the sugar.
3. Combine the flour, baking powder, salt, and vanilla and whisk into the egg mixture, along with the milk and melted butter.
4. Cut the apples into small pieces and mix with the cinnamon. Chop the caramels.
5. Distribute the batter into the cupcake liners and sprinkle the apples and candies over them. Bake on the oven's center rack for approximately 20 minutes. Allow to cool.

Topping

1. Beat the yogurt and cream with an electric mixer for about 5 minutes, until a creamy mixture forms.
2. Pipe or spread over the cupcakes and decorate with sugar flowers.

COCONUT and PASSION FRUIT CUPCAKES

Makes about 20 cupcakes

Fondant, also known as sugar paste, is a firm but pliable sugar icing that is used to cover and decorate cakes. It can be a little tricky to work with fondant, but the result looks really elegant. In order to make a design, roll out the sugar paste with a patterned rolling pin or a patterned silicone baking mat. Don't fill the cupcake liners with too much batter. To get a nice rounded lid, it helps if you put a generous layer of topping underneath.

Cupcakes

3 large eggs
$\frac{2}{3}$ cup granulated sugar
1 cup flour
$\frac{3}{4}$ cup sweetened, shredded coconut
1 teaspoon baking powder
$\frac{1}{4}$ teaspoon salt
$\frac{2}{3}$ cup natural low-fat yogurt
7 tablespoons butter, melted
Pulp of 2 whole passion fruits

Topping

3 tablespoons lemon juice
$\frac{1}{3}$ cup confectioner's sugar
10 oz. cream cheese
$\frac{1}{2}$ cup heavy cream

Decorations

9 oz. white fondant
Liquid or gel food coloring

Cupcakes

1. Preheat the oven to 350° F.
2. Mix the eggs with the sugar.
3. Combine the flour, coconut, baking powder, and salt, then whisk into the egg mixture along with the yogurt. Whisk in the melted butter and passion fruit pulp.
4. Divide the batter into the cupcake liners, leaving half an inch to the paper's edge. Bake on the center rack of the oven for approximately 20 minutes. Allow to cool.

Topping

1. Beat the lemon juice and confectioner's sugar into the cream cheese.
2. Using an electric mixer, add the cream and whip until fluffy.
3. Pipe a rounded top on each cupcake, slightly above the liner's edge.

Decoration

1. Dye the fondant the desired color by kneading food coloring into it.
2. Flatten the fondant about $\frac{1}{16}$ inch thick with a regular rolling pin, then roll it again with a patterned rolling pin. Punch out a circular top that is slightly larger than the cupcake and place on top of the topping. Serve the same day.

MINI-CUPCAKES WITH ROSE WATER AND GRAPEFRUIT

Makes about 20 mini cupcakes

I have an assistant named Miriam. She is wonderful and helps me with the things I don't have time for, like the shopping, baking, and prepping, and when I ran out of ideas, Miriam helped me finesse this sweet rose water and grapefruit pastry. Rose water can be overwhelmingly perfume-like if you overdo it, but just a drop can jazz things up nicely.

Cupcakes

1 large egg

⅓ cup granulated sugar

½ cup flour

½ teaspoon baking powder

¼ teaspoon salt

1 teaspoon vanilla sugar

1½ tablespoons milk

finely grated zest of 1 grapefruit

2 tablespoons freshly squeezed grapefruit juice

2 tablespoons butter, melted

1 teaspoon rose water

Topping

¼ cup confectioner's sugar

2 tablespoons freshly squeezed grapefruit juice

⅓ teaspoon rose water

A few drops of red food coloring

7 oz. cream cheese

¼ cup heavy cream

Decoration

Dried rose buds

Cupcakes

1. Preheat the oven to 350° F.
2. Mix the egg with the sugar.
3. Blend the flour, baking powder, salt, and vanilla sugar, then whisk into the egg mixture along with the milk, zest, and grapefruit juice. Whisk in the melted butter and rose water.
4. Distribute the batter in mini-cupcake liners. Leave at least ¼ inch to the paper's edge. Bake on the center rack of the oven for 10–15 minutes. Allow to cool.

Topping

1. Stir the confectioner's sugar, grapefruit juice, rose water, and food coloring into the cream cheese. Add the cream and whip with an electric mixer until fluffy.
2. Pipe the topping in a petal pattern with petal-shaped piping tip on the cupcakes. Decorate with dried rose buds.

TIP

To pipe flower-shaped toppings on cupcakes, you need a curved, petal-shaped tip. You can find videos online to see how this is done.

About Cake Pops

These cake pops are simply cake dough placed atop lollipop sticks and then decorated to your heart's desire. You crumble a cake mix with something sticky and good, such as peanut butter, chocolate, lemon curd, cream cheese, or hazelnut paste to make a stiff dough. The dough can be shaped into spheres, hearts, and other shapes, then dipped in chocolate.

If you don't have the time or desire to bake a cake for the pop, you can use the equivalent amount of store-bought chocolate muffins, pound cake, or brownies. Sticks for the pops can be purchased at hobby stores and online retailers that sell baking supplies. Or you can take wooden grilling skewers and cut them to the right length.

Although it is common to dip the cake in a candy melt (colored candy discs melted and then hardened to a sugar shell), you can use chocolate instead. It's best to start with white chocolate if you want to color it, and in most cases, don't hesitate to use ordinary food coloring. If you want your cake pops to have a stronger color, powder or gel colors work best. These dyes are fat-soluble and therefore work best with chocolate, which has a high fat content, as opposed to ordinary food coloring, which is water-soluble.

When decorating, you can use sprinkles, candy, melted chocolate, or anything that will taste and look good. For decorations like chicken wings, beaks, and claws, or a snowman's nose, I use something called mukhwas, which are Indian sugar-coated fennel seeds. They can be purchased at Indian grocery stores, but may be replaced with sprinkles or sugar paste in any shape and color you want.

Making certain cake pops can be quite involved and time-consuming. One solution is to bake the cake a day ahead, and enjoy it as it is, then make pops using the leftovers the next day. After you have dipped the cake pops, it's helpful to press the sticks into a piece of floral foam or Styrofoam, then allow them to solidify in the refrigerator. Keep your cake pops well-wrapped or in a tight container in the refrigerator for up to a week.

CAKE POPS WITH CHOCOLATE FILLING

Makes about 30 cake pops

Everything is more fun and playful when served on a stick!

Cake

½ *cup flour*

½ *cup cocoa*

1 teaspoon vanilla sugar

1 teaspoon baking powder

3 large eggs

¾ *cup granulated sugar*

7 tablespoons butter, melted

½ *cup milk*

Butter and dried plain bread crumbs for the pan

Dipping and Decoration

⅔ *cup peanut butter*

5 oz. white chocolate

5 oz. dark chocolate

Sprinkles and food coloring

Cake

1. Preheat the oven to 350° F.
2. Grease and crumb a pan that holds at least 2 quarts.
3. Mix the flour, cocoa, vanilla sugar, and baking powder together.
4. Using an electric mixer, beat the eggs and sugar until white and fluffy.
5. Sift the flour mixture into the egg mixture a little at a time, alternating with the melted butter and milk. Whisk gently together into a smooth batter.
6. Pour the batter into the pan and bake on the lower rack of your oven for about 35 minutes. Let cool a few minutes and then turn out the cake. Allow to cool completely.

Assembly

1. Pulse the cake into crumbs in a food processor. Add the peanut butter and blend together to form a thick batter.
2. Shape the mixture into hearts or round balls and insert a stick in each, attaching the sticks with a little melted chocolate. Allow to set in the fridge for about 30 minutes.
3. Carefully melt the chocolate for dipping in the microwave or over a water bath.
4. Dip each cake ball in a layer of chocolate. Let extra run off slightly, then decorate with sprinkles.
5. Stick the pop in a piece of floral foam or Styrofoam. Decorate with white chocolate that you've colored with a few drops of food coloring. Let them harden in the fridge.

Easter Cake Pops

Makes about 35 cake pops

Easter is my favorite holiday—bright, pastel, and candy-packed.
These cake pops are so sweet, they're almost too good to eat!

Cake

1 ½ cups flour

2 teaspoons baking powder

2 teaspoons vanilla sugar

3 large eggs

¾ cup granulated sugar

5 tablespoons butter, melted

⅔ cup milk

Butter and dried plain breadcrumbs for the pan

Dipping and Decoration

8 oz. lemon curd

7 oz. white chocolate

3 oz. milk chocolate

Yellow, red, green, and black food coloring

Sprinkles and mukhwas (see p. 62)

Sliced, blanched almonds

Cake

1. Preheat the oven to 350° F. Grease and crumb a pan that holds at least 2 quarts.
2. Mix the flour, baking powder, and vanilla sugar together.
3. Using an electric mixer, beat the eggs and sugar until fluffy.
4. Sift the flour mixture into the egg mixture a little at a time, alternating with the melted butter and milk. Whisk gently together into a smooth batter.
5. Pour the batter into the pan and bake on the oven's lower rack for about 40 minutes. Turn the cake upside down on parchment paper or a cooling rack, let cool a few minutes, and then remove the pan. Allow to cool completely.

Assembly

1. Pulse the cake into crumbs in a food processor. Add the lemon curd and blend together to form a thick batter.
2. Shape the mixture into round balls, eggs, and bunny heads and insert a stick in each in each, attaching the sticks with a little melted chocolate. Allow to set in the fridge for about 30 minutes.
3. Carefully melt the chocolates for dipping in the microwave or over a water bath.

Chicks

1. Dip the balls in a layer of white chocolate dyed with a few drops of yellow food coloring, and attach mukhwas (or sprinkles) as wings and beak. Insert the stick in a piece of floral foam or Styrofoam and let harden in the fridge. Paint the eyes with a toothpick dipped in black food coloring or with dark chocolate.

Easter Eggs

1. Dip the egg-shaped pops in white chocolate. Color a bit of the chocolate, then pipe as decoration for the eggs. Decorate with sprinkles if you like.

Easter Bunnies

1. Dip the bunny-shaped pops in milk chocolate. Add the almonds as ears and attach sprinkles for the nose. Pipe a mouth with melted white chocolate that you have colored pink. Paint the eyes with a toothpick dipped in black food coloring or some dark chocolate.

CHRISTMAS CAKE POPS

Makes about 35 cake pops

Cake

1 cup flour

1 ½ teaspoons baking powder

1 tablespoon mixed ground cinnamon, cloves, and ginger

3 large eggs

¾ cup granulated sugar

5 tablespoons butter, melted

⅔ cups sour cream, milk, or sour milk

Butter and dried plain bread crumbs for the pan

Dipping and Decoration

5 oz. cream cheese

½ to 1 cup lingonberry jam

12 oz. white chocolate

1 oz. dark chocolate

Sprinkles, candy pieces, and mukhwas (see p. 62)

Red food coloring

Cake and Assembly

1. Preheat the oven to 350° F. Grease and crumb a pan that holds at least 2 quarts.
2. Mix the flour, baking powder, and spices together.
3. Using an electric mixer, beat the eggs and sugar until fluffy.
4. Sift the flour mixture into the egg mixture a little at a time, alternating with the melted butter and sour cream. Whisk gently together into a smooth batter.
5. Pour the batter into the pan and bake on the oven's lower rack for 40–45 minutes. Turn the cake upside down on parchment paper or a cooling rack, let cool a few minutes, and then remove the pan. Allow to cool completely.
6. Pulse the cake into crumbs in a food processor. Add the cream cheese and pulse to combine; add jam, a little at a time, blending, until it forms a thick batter that will hold its shape when rolled.

Pops

1. Shape the mixture into cubes, conical hats, and small and large spheres and insert a stick into each one except the smaller balls, attaching the sticks with a little melted chocolate. Allow to set in the fridge for about 30 minutes.
2. Carefully melt the white chocolate in the microwave or over a water bath.

Snow Balls

1. Dip the balls in white chocolate and white sprinkles.

Presents

1. Dip the cube-shaped pops in white chocolate. Pipe string made from white chocolate that you have colored with a little red food dye.

Santa Claus Hats

1. Dip the hat-shaped pops in white chocolate that you have colored red. Place a large sprinkle or candy ball on the top as the tuft and pipe white chocolate along the hat's lower edge. Cover the edge with sprinkles.

Snowmen

1. Dip the small balls for the head in white chocolate and attach sprinkles or mukhwas as noses. Let harden in the fridge. Dip the larger balls attached to the stick in white chocolate, and fasten the heads on top with additional white chocolate. Let harden, then pipe on buttons and eyes using dark chocolate and attach candy pieces as a hat and scarf.

TIP

Instead of meringue filling, you can use marshmallow from a jar, canned whipped cream, or any cupcake topping.

WHOOPIE PIES

Makes about 35 double-layered cookies

You may think that whoopie pies are a trendy new cookie, but they've been around since the 1920s, and may have Amish origins. The cookie consists of two soft bases with a fluffy meringue filling in between. My version uses Italian meringue, which means that you add a shot of hot sugar syrup to the whipped egg whites.

Cookies

½ stick butter, room temperature

¼ cup canola oil

1 cup granulated sugar

1 large egg

2 teaspoons vanilla sugar

1½ cups flour

¾ cup cocoa

1½ teaspoons baking powder

½ teaspoon salt

1 cup milk

Meringue Filling

3 large egg whites

⅓ cup water

2 cups granulated sugar, divided

½ teaspoon vanilla powder or 2 teaspoons vanilla sugar

Decoration

Sprinkles (optional)

Cookies

1. Preheat the oven to 400° F.
2. Using an electric mixer, beat together the butter, oil, and sugar until fluffy. Mix in the egg and vanilla sugar.
3. Sift the flour, cocoa, baking powder, and salt together and whisk into the egg mixture a little at a time, alternating with the milk. Whisk gently together into a smooth batter.
4. Pipe or form the batter into mounds on a parchment paper-lined baking sheet and bake on the center rack of the oven for about 10 minutes. Allow to cool.

Meringue Filling

1. Put the egg whites into a clean, dry bowl (preferably stainless steel).
2. Bring the water and 1½ cups sugar to a boil in a saucepan with a thermometer and heat until 250° F. Do not stir or touch.
3. When the syrup has boiled for a little while, begin whisking the egg white with an electric mixer. When the meringue starts to become fluffy, whisk in the remaining ½ cup granulated sugar and continue whipping to a stiff meringue.
4. When the syrup reaches 250° F, pour it in a steady, thin stream into the meringue, whisking constantly. Add the vanilla powder and continue whisking for 5–10 minutes, until the meringue has cooled.
5. Pipe a dollop of meringue on half the cookies to create the bottom layers, then place together with the remaining cookies to assemble the whoopie pies. Dip the edges in sprinkles if desired. The cookies can be stored at room temperature for 3–4 days, or can also be frozen.

CHOCOLATE BALLS
WITH COFFEE LIQUEUR

Makes 25–30 balls

Using Kahlúa instead of coffee in chocolate balls gives them a grown-up twist.

7 tablespoons butter, room temperature
½ cup granulated sugar
1 tablespoon vanilla sugar
3 tablespoons cocoa
1¼ cups rolled oats
3 tablespoons Kahlúa or other coffee liqueur
Pearl sugar

1. Blend together all the ingredients until smooth.
2. Roll the mixture into small balls and dip them in pearl sugar. Let them harden in the fridge. Chocolate balls will last at least 1–2 weeks.

PETITS FOURS

Makes about 35 small petits fours

*Petits fours may vary in taste and appearance, but are always delicate miniature tarts.
These consist of shortbread cups filled with creamy lemon curd and decorated
with red currants. To bake the shortbread shells, you'll need mini tart molds,
available at well-stocked kitchen supply stores.*

Shortbread

   1 cup flour

   ¼ cup granulated sugar

   ¼ teaspoon salt

   7 tablespoons chilled butter

   1 large egg yolk

Lemon Curd

   *½ cup freshly squeezed lemon juice (the equivalent
of about 1–2 lemons)*

   4 tablespoons butter, finely diced

   ⅓ cup granulated sugar

   2 large eggs

Decoration

   Red currants

Shortbread

1. Preheat oven to 400° F.
2. Put the shortbread ingredients into a food processor and pulse into a dough. You can also knead the dough by hand.
3. Sprinkle a thin layer of flour over the mini-molds and fill them with the dough, either by simply pressing out an even layer of dough with your fingers; or by first rolling out the dough about ¹⁄₁₆ inch thick on a floured board and cutting them to fit. Set up the molds with space between them and put the dough over them. Press the dough into the shape and smooth the edges. Let stand in refrigerator for about 30 minutes.
4. Bake the shells on a baking sheet on the center rack of the oven for 8–10 minutes.

Lemon Curd

1. In a saucepan, heat the lemon juice, butter, and half the sugar. While that is heating, whisk together the eggs with the remaining sugar.
2. When the lemon juice mixture has come to a boil, whisk the egg mixture into it. Whisk thoroughly until the curd begins to thicken. Let the curd simmer on low heat for a minute, whisking often, then pull the pan from the heat and strain the custard through a very fine sieve to get it really smooth. Allow to cool.
3. Fill the shortbread shells with lemon curd. Chill in the fridge until firm. Garnish with red currants.

FROSTED SHORTBREAD COOKIES

Makes about 25 cookies

With a little patience and a steady hand, you can make cookies almost too pretty to eat!

Shortbread

1 cup flour

¼ cup granulated sugar

¼ teaspoon salt

7 tablespoons chilled butter

1 large egg yolk

Frosting

2 ½ cups confectioner's sugar

3–4 tablespoons water

1 tablespoon butter, room temperature

1 tablespoon honey

Liquid or gel food coloring

Decoration

Sprinkles

Shortbread

1. Preheat the oven to 400° F.
2. Put the ingredients for the shortbread in a food processor and pulse into a dough. You can also knead the dough by hand.
3. On a floured surface, roll out the dough ¹⁄₁₆ inch thick and cut cookies in the shapes of ice cream cones, umbrellas and the like.
4. Bake the cookies on the center rack of the oven for 8–10 minutes. Let cool.

Frosting

1. Mix all the ingredients for the frosting in a bowl. Whisk for a minute.
2. Divide the icing into several bowls and add food coloring to create your desired colors. Add a few drops of extra water if the frosting seems too thick.

Assembly

1. Decorate the cookies by first piping the frosting in thin strands along the contours of your design. Let dry for a minute and then pipe generously with icing to fill in the remaining surface. You may need to thin the glaze with a few extra drops of water when you fill the surfaces.
2. Decorate with sprinkles, and let the frosting dry for a few hours. The cookies can be stored in a jar at room temperature for 5–6 days.

NUTELLA SANDWICHES

Makes about 30 cookies

Nutella straight from the jar makes a quick and delicious filling for these chocolate cookies.

Cookies

2 sticks butter, chilled

3 ⅓ tablespoons granulated sugar

1 large egg yolk

1 ½ cups flour

6 rounded tablespoons cocoa

¼ teaspoon salt

Filling

7 ounces Nutella

Cookies

1. Preheat the oven to 400° F.
2. Mix the butter, sugar, and egg yolk in a food processor for a minute, until it becomes soft and white. Add the remaining ingredients and mix into a dough. You can also work the ingredients together in a bowl if you do not have a food processor.
3. Shape the dough into three long, thin rolls and cover them in plastic wrap. Let the dough rest in the refrigerator for at least 30 minutes so that it becomes firm enough to cut into slices.
4. Remove plastic wrap and cut the rolls into ¼-inch-thick slices. Place slices on parchment paper-lined sheets and bake on the center rack of the oven for 7–8 minutes. Allow to cool.

Assembly

1. Spread the Nutella on half of the cookies, then place together with the remaining cookies to create cookie sandwiches. They can be stored at room temperature for 3 days, or can be frozen.

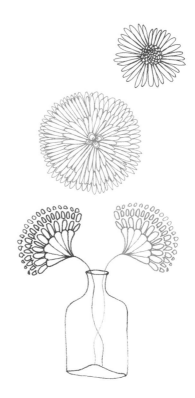

Raspberry Cookies

Makes 25–30 cookies

Delicate shortbread cookies with a heart of raspberry cream.
Place them in a beautiful tin and take to a picnic or dinner party.

Cookies

> 1⅔ cups flour
>
> ½ cup potato flour
>
> ¼ teaspoon salt
>
> 2 sticks chilled butter, diced
>
> ½ cup granulated sugar

Raspberry Filling

> About 1¼ cups raspberries
>
> 8 oz. white chocolate
>
> ¼ cup heavy cream
>
> A few drops of red food coloring (optional)

Cookies

1. Preheat the oven to 400° F. Mix the flour, potato flour, and salt in a bowl.
2. Add the cold butter and distribute it throughout the flour mixture with your fingertips. Quickly mix into a dough, then work in the granulated sugar. It is also possible make the dough in a food processor.
3. Wrap the dough in plastic wrap and let rest in refrigerator for at least 30 minutes. If it becomes too hard, just work with it a little on your countertop until it becomes pliable again.
4. Roll out the dough about ¹⁄₁₆ inch thick on a floured board. Cut disks using a round cookie cutter. Evenly space the cookies on a sheet lined with parchment paper. Punch a hole in the middle of half of the cookies. You can use an apple corer, piping tip, or small knife to do this.
5. Bake the cookies on the center rack of the oven for 7–8 minutes until they're light golden brown. Allow to cool.

Raspberry Filling

1. Puree the raspberries with a hand blender. Break the chocolate into small pieces.
2. Mix the raspberries, chocolate, and cream in a saucepan and heat gently on low heat until the chocolate has melted. Stir occasionally until you have a fairly smooth paste.
3. Add a few drops of red food coloring if you want it to be more pink. Let the cream cool and solidify a bit in the fridge.

Assembly

1. Spread or pipe the filling onto the cookies without holes, then place the cookies with holes on top. They can be stored for 2–3 days at room temperature, or frozen.

MADELEINES

Makes about 50 small cookies

Madeleine cookies are small, soft cookies that are usually baked in shell-shaped molds, and became famous after Marcel Proust wrote about them in his book In Search of Lost Time. Although most people don't realize this, the shell-shape is the cookie's underside. If you follow the correct French method, you'll get a large hump on the top, which one usually displays, but I'm a little rebellious and do the opposite.

2 large eggs
½ cup granulated sugar
Finely grated zest of ½ lemon
⅔ cup flour
½ teaspoon baking powder
7 tablespoons butter, melted
Butter for greasing the pan

1. Preheat the oven to 350° F. Grease the madeleine molds with a little butter.
2. Divide the eggs into yolks and whites, then whisk the yolks together with the sugar and lemon zest until very fluffy. Whisk the egg whites to firm peaks in a clean, dry bowl (preferably stainless steel).
3. Sift the flour and baking powder into the egg yolk batter, then stir in the butter. Gently fold the egg whites into the batter.
4. Fill two thirds of each mold with batter, preferably using a piping bag. Place the molds on a baking sheet or cooling rack and bake in the bottom of the oven for 12–15 minutes. The cookies should be lightly browned on top. Remove from the mold immediately. Eat the cookies the same day, or freeze.

TIP

Silicon or Teflon madeleine molds can be found in well-stocked cooking stores or online. If you don't have a lot of molds on hand for 50 small cookies, it's fine to bake the cookies in several batches. If you don't have special Madeleine molds feel free to use small muffin liners.

Strassburger Cookies

Makes about 20 cookies

These small, tasty bites melt in your mouth, and it's hard to eat just one. They're perfect for freezing and thawing in the blink of an eye, if you have guests over for coffee. Double the recipe if you want them to last for a while.

Cookies

9 tablespoons butter, room temperature

¼ cup confectioner's sugar

1 tablespoon vanilla sugar

½ cup potato flour

½ cup flour

⅛ teaspoon salt

Decoration

3 oz. dark chocolate

¼ cup chopped hazelnuts

Cookies

1. Preheat the oven to 350° F.
2. Put the butter, confectioner's sugar, and vanilla sugar into a food processor and mix together until white and fluffy.
3. Add the potato flour, flour, and salt and pulse into a dough.
4. Pipe evenly spaced, shell-shaped cookies on a parchment paper-lined baking sheet.
5. Bake on the center rack of the oven for 10-12 minutes or until cookies are slightly browned. Allow to cool.

Decorations

1. Carefully melt the chocolate in the microwave or over a water bath and dip half the cookies into the melted chocolate.
2. Sprinkle with chopped hazelnuts and let harden in the fridge. Store the cookies in the fridge or freeze them.

Tip

Piping the batter can be a bit tricky if you're not used to it. In order to facilitate the piping, it is important for the butter to be very soft. Better a little melted than too cold and hard. You need a heavy plastic piping bag and piping tip, or an old-fashioned canvas piping bag. Or you can simply roll the dough into balls and flatten with a fork.

Amaretti

Makes about 12 cookies

A crunchy little Italian pastry that goes perfectly with an espresso.
A relative of the macaron, but oh, so much simpler to bake!

1 cup packed almond paste
⅓ cup granulated sugar
1 large egg white
Scant ¼ teaspoon bitter almond flavoring / oil
1 tablespoon confectioner's sugar

1. Preheat the oven to 350° F.
2. Work the granulated sugar into the almond paste with your hands, then add the egg white a little at a time. Add the bitter almond flavor.
3. Roll small balls of dough and place evenly on baking sheets lined with parchment paper. Moisten your hands well with a little water to prevent the dough from sticking.
4. Flatten the cookies slightly. If you dry the cookies on the pan for about 2 hours before baking, then they'll crack neatly.
5. Pinch the cakes with your thumb and forefinger. Dust with a little confectioner's sugar and bake on the center rack of the oven for about 12 minutes. Allow to cool.

FUDGe CUPS

Makes 15–20 cups

Brush melted chocolate inside mini cupcake liners to make delicious pastry shells.

Chocolate Molds
6 oz. dark chocolate

Fudge
4 oz. dark chocolate
⅔ cup heavy cream
⅔ cup granulated sugar
2 tablespoons light corn syrup
5 tablespoons butter, room temperature

Decoration
Fresh, edible flowers, such as carnations (optional)

Chocolate Molds
1. Break the chocolate into pieces and carefully melt it in the microwave or over a water bath.
2. Brush a fairly thick layer of chocolate on the inside of the mini-cupcake liners, small cupcake liners, or cookie cutters. If you double up the paper liners, it will be easier. Allow the molds to solidify in the refrigerator for at least 30 minutes.
3. Brush any additional chocolate in the places where it looks thin, and let it harden for a while in the fridge. Carefully remove the paper liners and put the chocolate molds in the fridge again.

Fudge
1. Break the chocolate into small pieces and mix with the cream, sugar, and syrup in a saucepan. Bring to a boil, then simmer for a few minutes. Remove from the heat and stir in the butter. Allow to cool completely.
2. Pipe the fudge in the molds. Keep cold until serving. Decorate with edible flowers.

LInGoNbeRRY CUPS

Makes 15–20 cups

Tart lingonberry, fluffy cream, and sweet white chocolate—an unbeatable combination.

Chocolate Molds
6 oz. white chocolate

Lingonberry Cream
1 cup (4 oz.) lingonberries, fresh or frozen and thawed
1 tablespoon confectioner's sugar
¾ cup heavy cream

Decoration
Fresh, edible flowers, such as carnations (optional)

Chocolate Molds
1. Follow instructions 1–3 for fudge cups.

Lingonberry Cream
1. Mix the berries well with a hand blender, then stir in the confectioner's sugar.
2. Whip the cream until fluffy and then fold in the lingonberries.
3. Pipe the lingonberry cream into the molds. Decorate with edible flowers and serve immediately.

LaVENDER MEDaLLIeNS

Makes 15–20 medallions

These confections are as beautiful as small jewels. A little tartness from the lemon balances the sweet white chocolate and lavender. Dried lavender is sold in spice and tea shops.

Lavender Ganache

½ cup heavy cream

1 teaspoon honey

2 tablespoons lavender, fresh or dried

Finely grated zest of ½ lemon

5 oz. white chocolate

Blue and red food coloring

Lavender Sugar

1 tablespoon granulated sugar

1 tablespoon dried lavender

Blue and red food coloring

Chocolate Medallions

7 oz. white chocolate

Lavender Ganache

1. In a small saucepan, bring the cream, honey, lavender, and lemon to a boil. Remove from heat, cover with a lid, and let stand for about 20 minutes so the cream can absorb the flavors.

2. Meanwhile, finely chop the chocolate. Place in a bowl and then cover with a strainer.

3. Bring the cream to a boil again.

4. Pour the boiling hot cream through the strainer over the chocolate. Stir until it becomes a smooth ganache. Stir in a few drops of red and blue food coloring if you want a purple color for the ganache.

5. Pour the ganache in a piping bag and let cool in refrigerator for at least 2 hours.

Lavender Sugar

1. Pound the sugar and lavender finely with a mortar and pestle. Add a few drops of blue and red food coloring if you want the sugar to have a stronger purple color.

Chocolate Medallions

1. Melt the chocolate gently in the microwave or over a water bath.

2. Pipe out circles of chocolate on trays lined with waxed paper. Tap the pan on the table to flatten out the rounds.

3. Sprinkle lavender sugar over half of the disks and let them harden in the fridge.

4. Pipe filling onto the rounds without lavender sugar. Place a round with lavender sugar on top as a lid. Refrigerate until ready to serve.

MARBLED HAZELNUT BROWNIES

Makes about 30 small cakes

*The fancy marbled pattern on these little cakes is not as hard to create as you might think.
When coloring the white chocolate in this recipe, regular liquid food coloring isn't ideal.
In the absence of alternatives, it will still work, but powdered food coloring or
something similar will produce the best colors.*

Brownie

9 oz. dark chocolate, preferably 70% cocoa

2 sticks butter, room temperature

1¼ cups sugar

3 large eggs

1 large egg yolk

½ cup flour

½ cup cocoa

½ teaspoon baking powder

¼ teaspoon salt

½ cup hazelnuts, toasted and coarsely chopped

Frosting

9 oz. dark chocolate

9 oz. white chocolate

Red and green food dye, preferably powdered

Brownie

1. Preheat the oven to 350° F. Prepare an 8 x 10 inch baking dish, either with parchment paper or by greasing it.
2. Carefully melt 7 ounces of the chocolate over a water bath or in the microwave and let it cool a bit. Chop the remaining chocolate coarsely.
3. Using an electric mixer, beat the butter and sugar until soft and fluffy.
4. Add the eggs one at a time and yolk and whisk well between each addition. Stir the melted chocolate into the batter.
5. Combine the flour, cocoa, baking powder, and salt and sift into the batter. Mix until smooth, then carefully add the chopped chocolate and nuts. Pour the batter in the pan and smooth it to an even layer.
6. Bake on the center rack of the oven for 25–30 minutes. Test by using a toothpick. Some batter should cling to the toothpick, but the cake should not feel runny; however, it should not be completely baked through, either.
7. Let the cake cool, then cut into pieces.

Frosting

1. Carefully melt the dark chocolate and white chocolate separately in the microwave or over a water bath.
2. Color some of the white chocolate pink, some green, and keep some white.
3. Frost the brownie squares with a layer of dark chocolate. Drizzle stripes of white, pink, and green chocolate over the dark chocolate, then drag a toothpick through to create a marbled pattern. Let harden in the fridge. The squares can be stored in the refrigerator for 5–6 days.

INDEX

Thank You

Tremendous thanks to everyone who helped
with this book each in their different way!
Ulrika Pousette, Katy Kimbell, Eva Kruk, Miriam Parkman,
Maria Nilsson, Mia Gahne, Åsa Rickman,
Petronella Nilsson, Felicia Nyström, Anki Sörensen,
Annelie Wahlberg Leiwerth, Petra Grossman,
Tara Junker, Lisa Crafoord, Anders Lundkvist,
Elisabeth Pettersson, Gunnel Lindhult,
and Marie Abrahamsson.

MIA ÖHRN
Author

MIRIAM PARKMAN
Assistant

ULRIKA POUSETTE
Photographer